MW01119888

ONE HUNDRED POEMS FOR JESUS

A Personal Journey of Spiritual Healing and Discovery

Ned Jacob

xulon
PRESS

"With men this is impossible,
but with God all things are possible"
(Matthew 19:26)

For my children
Natalie, Andrew and Jonathan

TABLE OF CONTENTS

FOREWORD

Using Scripture as his touchstone, Ned Jacob shows you how to express your deepest feelings to God. He invites you to come along with him on a journey that will radically change your life as you discover the heart of God. On this personal journey Ned takes you inside the heart and mind of a man who at times seethed with intense emotions yet profoundly felt the presence of God.

Ned helps you to move beyond believing things about God - to actually sensing and experiencing His living presence. He teaches you not to be afraid of your feelings, but to view them as faith's great ally. He encourages you to take your feelings seriously, all feelings, to talk about them honestly, and relate to God intimately by means of them. These prayer poems will teach you how to navigate through trials such as suffering, insecurity, discouragement, doubt, and family problems. They will help you experience more fully the blessings of worship, finding forgiveness, freedom and healing.

On this journey of healing and discovery, Ned confesses again and again the intensity of his feelings, and invites you to empathize with them. But he never surrenders to mindless emotionalism. He consciously brings his feelings within the orbit of God's revealed character and will. In a day like ours, when the cultural tide forces us to identify emotional experience with spiritual experience, *One Hundred Poems* is a profitable corrective as the poems are guided by the Scriptures. I hope and pray that by the time you finish reading this wonderful book, your prayer would be like that of Ned Jacob's.

> *Give me Lord a heart of flesh*
> *And take away my heart of stone.*
> *For no one else can make that change,*
> *No one else but you alone.*

Habib Sakr, Youth Pastor
Chapel Place Presbyterian Church
Markham, Ontario

PREFACE

The Lord is good, and He is faithful. It all started from the time I packed away all my Christian books, tapes and CDs and put them in storage because I was angry with God. I thought that I deserved better from One whom I served for a long time, though not always faithfully, I must admit.

I had been a Christian for over twenty years and had for many years played drums in Sunday worship in various evangelical churches, mostly on a regular basis. However, the worship part had stopped making sense for me and I was contemplating resigning my music ministry.

Recently, I have been struggling with profound personal issues and was on the verge of giving up hope when I felt the hand of God intervene in an unexpected way.

One day I stopped at a traffic light and saw a car with a sticker advertising a Christian radio channel that I had not heard of before. I put on the radio to listen to this channel and I heard a preacher talk about Jonah. He said that one of the lessons of the book of Jonah was that if you run away from God, not only will you hurt yourself, but you will hurt others as well.

That was the first time I realized that God had a task for me to do. Not long after that, I attended a revival meeting. That night I went home, laid myself on the floor and said to God, "Lord, I cannot go lower than this. Please look down on your servant and help me to deal with this pain." Finally, I asked, "Lord, what is it that you want from me?"

Several days later, I was praying when something inside said, "One hundred poems." It was a faint but compelling voice. It was daunting too, so I quickly dismissed it as my own imagination. I had never written so many poems in my life. I had written about thirty poems in a span of twenty years, so this to me would be a formidable task by any stretch of the imagination.

But the voice was persistent. I said, "Lord, this is impossible. It cannot be done." Then I found myself writing the first poem, and then the second, all the while I was pouring my heart out to God. I found I was finishing one poem each day, and I was very surprised by the quality of the poems. Two months later I had written fifty poems. I had poured my heart out in these poems and each day there was new inspiration from God. However, I had exhausted all that I needed to say to God and, what is more, found that the last poem drew all the previous ones to a conclusion.

I was stuck. I still had another fifty poems to write and went several days without writing a single word. I had writer's block. It was very frustrating, especially since the inspiration had previously been coming on a daily basis. I prayed and prayed, but nothing came.

Soon after, God told me that I was now ready for my journey. Before I could go on this journey, He had wanted to heal me and equip me with the tools necessary to undertake the next step and to ensure that it was a success. The previous fifty poems had been the easy part. However, they were the biggest part because they were the most important one. God wanted me to take a journey with Him on a mountain, but I felt that now I would have to work much harder than before.

The inspiration resumed on a daily basis, once I realized that this was what God had in store for me. I had never once, while writing any of these poems, planned what I would be writing next. The details of the journey unfolded with each passing day, and each day was as exciting as the one before.

Finally, the daily inspirations led me to new and exciting discoveries about God. I tried to describe these faithfully in my poetry. There were some "Aha!" moments in the book, which for me came as a very pleasant surprise. In one instance, I had an inspiration that I never expected and did not understand its meaning, yet I found myself writing like I knew exactly what it meant. I really had to think hard about this one, but when I did, the answer was so simple and profound that it enabled me to finish the second part of the book and set the direction for the final part.

I invite the reader to share this journey with me and discover some of the qualities of God through the poetry that I was inspired to write. God asks us to do impossible things, and gives us the ability, power and perseverance to carry these tasks out. The whole book took just over four months to write. I attribute this amazing feat to Him alone and not to any wisdom or abilities on my part. In fact, this is how we can be sure that something is from God, in that He asks from us the impossible, and then enables us to do it.

The Lord is wonderful and faithful. And He is good.

Ned Jacob
Scarborough
August 2005

ACKNOWLEDGEMENTS

Recently, the Lord has been drawing my attention to a very important responsibility. Since I have completed a book about spiritual healing, He has impressed on my heart the task of using this book as a part of the continual healing process. It is for this reason that I have tried to be all inclusive of everyone who has helped me directly or indirectly in bringing this book to fruition.

First and foremost my deepest thanks go to the Lord who has demonstrated that all things in Him are possible, and that His promise to be with His children always, is accurate and true in every sense.

Next, I would like to thank my wife Reem and my children who have stood by me and encouraged me every step of the way and understood the sacrifices involved in writing these poems. I would also like to sincerely thank my extended family for supporting me whenever I needed a helping hand.

My deep gratitude goes out to the following persons for their prayers, encouragement and support.

From Chapel Place Presbyterian Church, Habib Sakr,

youth pastor; Makram Keriakis, church elder; Maged Girgis and Nady Boutros, worship leaders; Sameh Hanna, church elder and pastor-in-training, and Nevien Hanna; Makram Barsoum, church elder who is also with SAT7 satellite television Christian service, and Mona Barsoum.

From Toronto, Canada, Wafaa Wahba, Bayview Glen Church; Rev. Nizar Shaheen, founder of Light For All Nations; Yacoub and Samira Haddad; Ramzi and Sima Haddad; Samer and Samira Haddad; Dahlia Haddad; Fuad Haddad; Suad and Zaki Kharooba; Nabil and Sherine Kharooba; William and Siham Aweida; Joseph and Maha Faragalla ; Joe and Maha Girgis; Brian and Kathryn Holland; Rev. Chris and Marg Miller; Gerald Field; Amanda Waddell.

From Melbourne, Australia, Abdou and Judy Grace, Middle East Christian Outreach; Rev. Paul and Amal Kelada, Arabic Baptist Church.

Finally, I would like to thank my editor, Rudy Gafur, an author himself, for guiding me through the process that brought this work to completion.

PROLOGUE

Save me Lord for I am Yours,
And make my heart a burning flame.
Purify and guide my lips
To glorify Your holy name.

Give me Lord a heart of flesh,
And take away my heart of stone.
For no one else can make that change,
No one else but You alone.

Move me Lord the way You choose
So I can do Your will today.
Though it means I'll bear my cross
And walk behind You all the way.

Twenty Years Later ...

Part 1

THE HEALING

ONE

I lift up my eyes from my deepest despair,
I turn to the skies to see if You're there.
I seek Your presence in a silent prayer,
But You're not here or You no longer care.

You said a test of faith would be through fire
And to consider it a joy in times of trial.
But this is one fire I can sure do without
And the joy I should feel has not come about.

So to the heavens above I raise my hand
When all I can say is I don't understand.
Just confess my sins and depend on Your grace
Then plead for the presence of Your kindly face.

TWO

If You are my loving Father
Why is my heart filled with fear?
If I'm Your beloved son
Why has my heart lost all cheer?
Why do I then feel like an orphan,
Unloved and forsaken,
That my faith has been tested
And found severely shaken?

Until when will You keep away
Your merciful grace from me?
Is there something I should learn
Or something I do not see
Or will You tell me if I ask You
So You can help me to know,
What Your will is for me,
How You can help me to grow?

So have mercy on Your servant
As I fall down on my knees;
As I seek Your forgiveness
And You listen to my pleas.
And I long for Your gentle voice
Telling me I'm a forgiven son.
In return I will praise Your name
And say Your will be done.

THREE

Lord I thank You for the trials
That You allow me to go through,
For it's in times like these I am
Able to grow in You.
It's in times like these I know
You are closer to me,
And I hold on to Your promises
You'll embrace me gracefully.

Even though the darkness
Has gained the upper hand,
Though agents of the enemy
Have occupied more land,
And hope is fading that now I can
Barely see the light,
Your hand will be guiding me
All through the night.

Then I know that there's a time
When there will come a dawn;
That is the time when I know
To a new faith I'll be born.
Then the darkness will disappear
And I will see You more clearly,
For I'll know You are with me
And I will love You more dearly.

FOUR

Help me Lord that I may have
The faith that knows no fear;
Faith that knows with certainty
That You are always here;
Faith of a child when his father
Takes and holds his hand,
Though the child knows not his fate
Nor he can understand.

I wish that I were able
To comprehend Your ways;
To rely on Your protection
For the remainder of my days.
I just want to thank You Lord
That You are here to stay;
That You'll help me through the fire
And deliver me, come what may.

In the stillness of the night,
I pour my heart to You
And pray that You will guide me
And help me to get through.
Though everything seems so hopeless
I know You're still my friend,
Who'll always be with me,
For days that never end.

FIVE

When those who are my friends
Have all forsaken me;
When life takes me to a destination
I can no longer see.
When the current grows ever so strong
And pulls me from the shore,
My faith will grow even stronger still
As I wait at Your door.

Sometimes all You ask of me
Is to be still and wait,
And I pray to You in my solitude
As I sit at Your gate.
When I am in Your perfect love
That is utterly pure,
Then in Your timing that's exact
I am completely sure.

For then I'm able to rejoice
You'll deliver me one day,
From the hands of my enemies
Who are standing in my way.
For the darkness will surely break
To the brightness of the morning,
And I will bathe in the warmth
Of Your love that is flowing.

SIX

It's Your presence around me
That makes my life so sweet;
It's Your spirit inside me
That makes my soul complete.
Your guidance gives me hope
In the middle of the darkness,
And Your love fills my heart
To the brink with gladness.

It's Your assurance that
Takes away all of my fears.
You promised that You would
Wipe away all of my tears,
And I depend fully on You
For every passing day,
That You will help me to deal with
What it brings my way.

You never promised that life would be
Such a happy affair;
You promised You won't let me take
More than I can bear.
If this would help me to become
Ever more like You,
Then I accept what Your hand
Is preparing me to do.

SEVEN

You are the potter; I am the clay,
You're my provider, come what may.
You are my strength
When the wind blows strong;
My beacon in the night
No matter how long.

You're the song in my heart
That helps me to be cheerful;
My guide in the wilderness
So now I'm never fearful;
My comforter when my castles
Begin to tumble down;
My healer when I sin,
For Your mercies abound.

You are my rock that keeps me
On a steady ground,
When dark coloured clouds
Come gathering around.
You are my destination
When it's time to say goodbye
From this world of sorrows,
When I'm appointed to die.

EIGHT

How can I ever thank someone
Who has cured my blindness
And who has always shown me
His never-ending kindness?
How can I then worship a God
That is mighty and strong,
When I've been nothing but a rebel
And a sinner all along?

Why would this God love me
Or want to die for me,
So I can live all my days
With Him in eternity?
Why would He even want
To listen to my prayer
Or show interest in me,
Or even want to care?

Yet this is what You did;
You died for me on the cross.
That's because You couldn't bear
To see me at a loss.
And You would listen to my prayer
To Your heart's delight,
Even if I were to talk to You,
All through the night.

NINE

When the world doesn't know
Where to turn to look for love,
All I do is turn my eyes
Up towards the heavens above.
For it is there that I find
The source of all that is good,
Though why You'd love one like me
I never understood.

Even though Your loving hand
Sometimes goes down with force,
I can rest in the assurance
That I am always Yours.
And it is then I know I am,
For sure, Your beloved son
When Your will in my life
Is required to be done.

Then I grow in Your knowledge
In the mystery of Your ways,
And I grow closer to You
For the remainder of my days.
And I thank You for keeping me
From the road that is wide,
That leads in due course to the grieving
Of Your spirit inside.

TEN

Unworthy, that's me, though You came
From the sky, for me, to die;
Worthy You are, the Lamb of God,
Even though I do not know why,
You would shed Your blood willingly,
To wash my sins completely;
My penalty to pay,
An eternity beside You to guarantee.

All my being is crying out
In thankfulness to You,
And so I call Your name out loud
For the things that You do.
And all I care about from this world
Would only be one thing.
What service I can offer or what
To Your throne I can bring.

For when at the end of my days
When from this life I will depart.
My Saviour and me, together at last,
Never again we'll be apart.
And I will forever to eternity be
Spending all my days,
Serving and also praising Him,
Giving Him thanks for all His ways.

ELEVEN

If I were listening to what
You had wanted to tell me;
If I had paid attention to what
You were trying to say,
I would not then have found myself
In this mess I am in,
But this time I know I'd chosen
To learn the hardest way.

Forgive me if I failed in what
You wanted me to do;
For also taking some actions
That failed to honour You.
And now I am at such a loss
In a distant and a foreign land,
Without Your guidance or Your grace,
Or Your loving hand.

So I pray that You restore me
To my preceding place;
Close to the side where surely I
Can depend on Your grace.
And I pray that I will listen
And then not move ahead,
Without You, so it's not my will,
But Your will instead.

TWELVE

When it's hard to forgive those
Who have caused my pain,
And have rendered my best efforts
To become lost in vain.
When my enemies at the door
Revel in my disgrace,
It's at that moment that I do
Seek out Your holy face.

When my pain becomes so strong
That it's too much to bear.
When I feel that I was cheated
That life has never been fair.
When all of what I want to do
Is draw back from it all,
And I feel I've been defeated
I can never again walk tall.

Then I remember the many times
That You had forgiven me;
When I didn't deserve to be loved
By any small degree,
And that they crucified You when
You were the righteous One.
Just so that You can make of me
Your forgiven son.

THIRTEEN

You said that they would hate me
For no reason at all,
Just the way they hated You
And planned for Your fall.
And that they'd make a lot of fun
Of what I do stand for,
Just the way they mocked what You
Tried to tell them before.

So then if they have hated me
It's because I am Your son,
A matter of fact relationship
That could never be undone.
In this I take heart and I know
There is no need to run,
For in this battle I do know
Which side has already won.

So I can walk tall in the face
Of what people might say,
And live my life in anticipation
For that single day
When You will then come back to take us
To our brand new place
In heaven, where we'll fix our eyes
On Your holy face

FOURTEEN

In Your blood I am protected
And all my sins have been forgiven;
In Your palm I am assured
That my full name has been written.
In Your truth I am immersed
Now it's clearer I can see;
In Your freedom I am delighted
That I am now truly free.

In Your peace I am contented
So that I have no more fears;
In Your promises I am secure
That You will wipe away my tears.
In Your love I am surrounded
So that I am never forsaken;
In Your grace I am fulfilled
And all my weaknesses have been taken.

In Your spirit I am bathed
So now I know You are the One;
In Your presence I am kept
That's how I know I am Your son.
In Your holiness I am awed
So I also have the fear of the Lord;
In Your glory I'll be forever
Where I will take my reward.

FIFTEEN

As long as You are holding my hand
I will not slip or fall;
As long as I am on Your shoulders
I will be walking tall.
As I rest my head on Your gracious breast
I know I am protected;
When I lay me down at Your feet
I know I'm not rejected.

Even before I was made in the womb
You called me by my name;
Cloaked me with Your righteousness
And took from me my shame.
You cleansed me with Your blood
That was shed on the cross for me;
You raised me up much high above
Rough land or stormy sea.

And now You stand at my defence
As You gently plead my case;
You soothe me as a father would
My troubles You embrace.
You take me up on higher ground
Just when I'm broken down;
When pride is lost that's when You say
Come now receive your crown.

SIXTEEN

You look for workers in Your kingdom
To those who have been broken.
With an eager heart they seek You,
Not just a meagre token.
To all of those who take their cross
With gladness in their hearts,
With little regard to each sacrifice
That can tear their lives apart.

You look for those who love You
And have love for one another,
Who love the members of Your body
As a sister or as a brother.
Those who submit to Your power
And ask that You give them wisdom,
Your glory is their sole intention
When working for Your kingdom.

I pray You'll make a disciple of me
And a member of these workers,
That Your servant then be chosen
As one of the peacemakers.
And just as soon as You are finished
With the refinement of my ways,
I'll be in Your service joyfully
For the remainder of my days.

SEVENTEEN

I quiet down my heart
In preparation for my supplication,
I fall down on my knees in awe
As I pray for restoration.
I call out on Your holy name
To bring forth Your salvation,
And heal us as Your own people
And as a divided nation.

Help us to always keep in mind
The passion of our former love,
The day we called You "Father,"
A gift that is from up above.
And when this love is rectified
And grows to be a burning flame,
The answer will come to those who pray
And call upon Your holy name.

EIGHTEEN

Have you ever felt that your heart was so light
Or seen stars twinkle brighter than bright?
Have you ever felt like a bird soaring high
That you long to reach out and touch the sky?

Have you ever smiled on a wet, rainy day
Or trifled and laughed the hours away?
Have you ever perceived a rainbow so near
Or ever found courage and had nothing to fear?

Has your soul ever been so full of grace
That beauty and love in your heart had a place?
That suddenly you found the answer to it all
And finally found harmony within your soul?

If ever you have felt this way before;
If ever you were saved from a distant shore;
If ever He has come to live in your heart,
You will then have found what love is about.

NINETEEN

Without You my life is a worthless pantomime,
Or maybe like a poem whose words do not rhyme.
Like a lost soul in the desert with no place to hide,
A tree leaf that has long shrivelled up and dried.

Without You there's just no meaning for laughter,
A life with a sentence of sadness ever after;
Without You it's hard to just keep on smiling,
And no reason for the sun to even keep on shining.

TWENTY

I am just a fleeting tourist
Passing through this foreign land,
And I fully know that its end
Is now becoming close at hand.
For as it was in the days of Noah
They mocked and would not listen,
You will come as a thief in the night
The way it has been written.

In a blink of an eye Your own are gathered
Then they will be taken,
And they will abide evermore with You
No more to be forsaken.
And then they'll see for the very first time
Your glory that is clear,
And they will find their peace in You
Now that You are near.

As a citizen of a heavenly place
I will gladly bear all pain,
For it's only for a little while longer
Till You come again.
And then I will be with my Saviour
And my trusted friend,
And live in the warmth of His love
Days that never end.

TWENTY ONE

Lord I present my life to You
As one living sacrifice,
So that I am not afraid
If called upon to pay the price
Of discipleship to You
And all that this would signify:
Rejection, scorn or whatever else
That people will imply.

For no one can be better than
The Master that one serves,
And also no one should receive
Any more than one deserves.
Except by grace You call us friends
And friends are there to share,
The secrets of the kingdom that
To us You have laid bare.

The secrets that were disguised
From men throughout the ages,
Were written in Your Holy Book
In the chapters of its pages.
Unless like children we become
We shall never understand,
The secrets of Your Holy Book
And the future that's at hand.

TWENTY TWO

Tell me please what it is
You would like me to express,
But before I come to Your presence
This I want to confess.
That I am finding it hard to maintain
My full focus on You,
And learn from You what it is
That You would like me to do.

Is there anything special Lord
That You would like me to say?
Am I in Your perfect will
Or should I pursue another way?
Here I am an open book
Use me Lord to spread Your word,
And tell the story of Your love
To those who have never heard.

That this is only about You Lord
Help me then to contemplate,
Here I am present at Your feet
Your holy commandments I await.
Guide my thoughts and my pen
For my own success is not my aim,
But so that I can praise You Lord
And glorify Your holy name.

TWENTY THREE

Sometimes I feel a longing towards
All the things that I have lost,
My refusal to bargain with my faith
Burdens me with an enormous cost.
And I do sometimes ask myself
Why God would allow such a loss,
Then I remember that I did declare
I am ready Lord to bear my cross.

You took me away and enrolled me
In the academy of heaven,
A different kind of learning
Where no prestige is given.
And only when the ego has
Completely been extinguished,
Then one receives a high reward
And grows to be distinguished.

TWENTY FOUR

His God has surely deserted him,
That's what some might say,
And some might also ponder that
My faith in God has gone astray.
But they do not know that I am
Right now in the midst of the fire,
That God allows in order that
He could lift my faith much higher.

Don't gloat over me, my enemies,
When I fall I can then arise again,
For now there's another inside the fire
To help me get through my pain.
And I will come out purified
With the guidance of His holy hand,
For He promised that He will not allow
For more than I could stand.

And my friends, they all want to give me
Some of their good advice.
They don't know the wisdom of Your ways
That You have as a device.
My enemies now I have forgiven
And from now on I shall resort,
To the designs of Your hands
And to the justice of Your heaven's court.

TWENTY FIVE

Do not give me too much gain
Lest I keep You out of my life,
Too little else I turn to another
Should I go through times of strife.
Just Your daily bread so that
I can always depend on You,
And plenty of Your grace so that
You can help me make it through.

Help me to build my treasure where
It could never lose its colour,
Guide me that I live my life
In deeds that give You honour.
Never let me think it was
My wisdom that won the day,
And help me put my trust in You
That You'll always lead the way.

TWENTY SIX

Lord I am so undeserving
Of the daily mercies You provide,
And sometimes from Your awesome presence
I feel I want to hide.
But in Your blood I'm justified
As I enter into Your holy place,
Without the protection of Your blood
I could never be near Your face.

Thank You Lord for letting me know
That I'm Your special son,
I thank You for Your spirit in me
That declares You are the One.
Sometimes I'm so overwhelmed
Of Your special love for me,
Sometimes I just cannot wait
Till I serve You eternally.

TWENTY SEVEN

I love You Lord with all my heart
With all my strength and soul,
Each part of me cries out to You
Please Lord accept my all.
I praise You for Your constant love
All that You've done for me,
The Alpha and Omega has opened my eyes
Now I can clearly see.

Love your neighbour as yourself
This, Lord, You have commanded.
Forgive your enemies; bless them too,
No less You have demanded.
So help me Lord that I fulfil
This part of Your instruction,
As by example You explained
At Your shameful crucifixion.

TWENTY EIGHT

When a stronger warrior I became
In the battle for Your kingdom,
From heaven I looked for guidance,
Gave up all earthly wisdom,
When I started to repossess the land
That was stolen by the enemy,
The attacks just came, fast and strong,
From all that was surrounding me.

I'm now a stronger fighter
In the battle of the ages,
Between the redeemed and the evil one
That till this day it rages.
But as it is in a foreign realm
It is so simple not to see,
The battle for deliverance
That is fought for you and me.

But You my God are my shield
So I shall fear no wickedness,
As long as I am in Your will
I'm protected by Your holiness.
Then all of those redeemed by blood
Shall see a mighty victory,
When in the end the Lamb will bind
The hands of our adversary.

TWENTY NINE

The sweetest period of the day
Is when I sit down by Your side,
And I calm down in Your presence
From the peace that wells inside.
I lay my burdens at Your feet
Where You said that they belong,
And offer You praises in the night,
Honour You all day long.

It's better still when I hear You call
Inviting me to Your holy place,
Where then Your blood is my shield
I receive Your endless grace.
I feel enclosed by Your love
That prods and then permeates my soul,
And a perfect father You become
Who never wants to let me fall

THIRTY

Your word in Your Holy Book
Is the letter of love You wrote for me,
Written with Your guiding hand
And addressed to me personally.
You knew me even before the world
Was put together by Your hands,
Gave me my abilities so
You could include them in Your plans.

You write to me of Your endless love
And all of what this could bring,
When I serve with a contented heart
No other but my gracious King.
But should I follow a foreign god
I hear this warning in Your voice,
Then You would take my peace away
For You will have no other choice.

So help me Lord that I should be
A true and faithful son to You,
Help me fix my eyes on You
In everything that I say or do.
Help me that I daily read
And also that I know Your word,
To treasure every word from You
All of what I've read or heard.

THIRTY ONE

When my day becomes so hectic
That I don't have the time to rest,
And when I am giving my all
And believe I am running my best;
When my thoughts of current plans
Take priority above all things,
And then I wrestle with tomorrow
And all the new things that it brings.

That is the time when in the end
I drop down on my knees,
And call upon Your holy name
That You listen to my pleas;
To lift my eyes from the world
And fix them on the cross;
To also know that without You Lord
All things would be a loss.

THIRTY TWO

What does it mean to be successful
Some people might wonder and say?
How can then success be defined
Compared to the standards of the day?
Is it the man with the biggest house
Or the largest group of grown up toys?
Is it the woman who shops the most,
The one on the list of the famous boys?

Upon princes You pour contempt,
Upon the things not part of Your plans.
Loving the world dishonours Your ways
And derides the works of Your hands.
Your commandment is to love You
And receive in return the joy that You give,
To love our neighbour as ourselves
And learn from You how to forgive.

The truth about success is that
When seen from Your point of view,
We are judged by what extent
In Your image we are shaped like You.
So help me that I may reflect
More and more of Your holy face,
Though it means I'm cleansed by fire
Your cross of shame I shall embrace.

THIRTY THREE

When the enemy launches at me
His flaming hot arrows of doubt;
When he makes me insecure
Of what Your nature is all about.
I go back to Your Holy Book
To the promises that You give to me,
And have assurance of my worth
From the way You died to set me free.

And when the enemy declares to You
It's in the blessings that You provide;
That makes me want to call Your name
And always want to take Your side.
You go and hide from me Your face
All good things from me You take,
And then I'm filled with wonderment
Of this misfortune and my ache.

But I am steadfast, Oh my Lord,
In my trust and in my love to You,
For I believe in Your plans for me
In all the things You say or do.
And I am sure the dawn will rise
When truly I will have seen Your face,
And that You shall restore my pride
And take from me all my disgrace.

THIRTY FOUR

It's not only a matter of my faith in You
That You had wanted to test,
Or that You're shaping the jar of clay
Though I dare not to protest.
But that You want me to draw ever so
Closer to Your magnificent love,
So that I would receive all blessings
And power from the heavens above.

I need to admit, Oh my Lord,
That this is when I'm closer to You;
This is the time that I want to obey
All that You would expect me to do.
And if I later would look back
It's these days that I cherish the most,
Even though they are full of pain
And do come at a tremendous cost.

THIRTY FIVE

When I can't give thanks for daily things
That don't appear to be going well;
When my own destination is still unknown
Which road to follow I can barely tell.
I start to count the little things
That You've provided throughout the years,
And realize that the days of plenty
Have overcome the moments of tears.

"A tiny instance I have left you,"
Says the Lord of heaven and earth,
"In a time of anger," says the Lord,
"But you have a significant worth."
"I died for you," He then continues,
"So you'll always be by My side,
And I gave you the Holy Spirit so
You'll always preserve the joy inside."

Now I shift my focus towards the giver
Not on the gifts that He provides,
My view is then completely altered
When to the cross my gaze He guides.
I fall down on my knees in awe
With a heart that is so full of praise,
And I pledge that I will be His own
And worship Him, all of my days.

THIRTY SIX

When contentment from earthly riches
Can barely satisfy the hungry soul,
When the world is crying for some peace
With nobody found to heed the call.
It's You alone who can fulfil
The deepest desires of the heart,
And You alone who can provide
The peace the world cannot impart.

The living water flows from Your side
To quench my longing however deep,
You said You are the bread of life
Which You freely give for my soul to keep.
The way to heaven that is through You
Is the narrow but the single way,
And beside You till eternity
That is the place I desire to stay.

THIRTY SEVEN

I become scared when You are silent
Like a child who is lost in the night,
Like an infant without his mother
Or one who's given up the fight.
And I hunger for Your gentle voice
Giving me comfort in my despair,
While the Holy Spirit guides me and then
Also bonds with me in prayer.

The distance at which You stay from me
Is it due to a sin in my heart?
Or is it the focus on myself
That's keeping You silent on Your part?
I pray You will reveal to me
The reason for this deep distress,
Whether it's because of excessive pride
Or a hidden sin I need to confess.

THIRTY EIGHT

Instant forgiveness feels so sweet
When I come to You with a repentant heart,
And I have the promise in Your grace
That Your spirit in me will never depart.
And should I desire against or grieve
Or even resist Your spirit inside,
With a broken heart I come to You
And discover You're here by my side.

Give me Lord spiritual eyes
That I see sin the way You do
So I would not quench nor resist
The spirit that draws me closer to You.
And make me a mirror to reflect Your love
To those unable yet to see,
The power that's in Your sacrifice
And how You're able to set them free.

THIRTY NINE

I was an orphan when You picked me up
Desperate, dirty and dejected,
I was a slave to the lying one
Who made me think I was rejected.
Then You arrived and paid my price
Bestowed on me a brand new name,
Adopted me as Your beloved son
And cleansed all traces of my shame.

So how can I ever thank the One
Who took me out of the darkest pit?
And took me up to higher grounds
Where next to His throne I will sit.
And I will sing the praises of Him
Who's now the owner of my soul,
The One who bought me with His blood
To whom I will now give my all.

FORTY

Sometimes when I've sinned against You
And my sin is just too much to bear,
All day I feel low down and weary
That I fall down on my knees in prayer.
When forgiveness comes I'm not convinced
That I am now unsoiled and free,
I ask for more and You discern
That still for now I'm on my knee.

When I say that it's the second time
I've committed a sin against You Lord,
Which also means an urgent need
To come to the cross and be restored.
That's when You say You do not recall
My previous iniquities any more,
And all past times have been wiped out
And duly cast on a distant shore.

FORTY ONE

Lord I come to You with my questions
Not expecting an answer from You,
For Your thoughts are higher than mine
Your ways different in all that You do.
I simply trust in Your perfect ways
In the plan You have designed for me,
And know for sure You'll get me there
To my brand new home in eternity.

And when I'm there I'll have the time
To listen as You try to explain,
The reason for my suffering
Why You permitted all my pain.
And then for all eternity long
I'll try to fathom some of Your ways,
Where then I'll be a student to You
While You teach me for the rest of my days.

FORTY TWO

A closer walk with You Oh Lord
Is what my hungry heart desires,
A deeper knowledge of Your word
Is what my thirsty soul requires.
A humble acceptance of Your ways
Is what allows me to persevere,
A fervent faith in Your goodness
Is what reveals that You are near.

Though I might feel as if I've been
Abandoned and forsaken,
And though at times I feel lost
In the road that I have taken,
And sometimes I even wonder if
At certain times You care at all,
I trust when I am in Your will
That's when I'll never fall.

FORTY THREE

Your Holy Book is my faithful map
I use when I need to find the way;
My reassurance in testing times
When it's hard to find the will to pray.
The reminder of the promises You give
To those who call upon Your name,
The transformer of obstinate hearts
That can never be, or remain the same.

It's a sprinkling of the purest water
To those in need of a helping hand,
Or an infinite ocean to those who wish
That they could understand.
It's a letter of love sent to the bride
Who's eagerly waiting for her king,
And dreaming of that blissful day
And all the gifts her groom will bring.

FORTY FOUR

There will not be any turning back
To the old ways that I used to know,
Though life can sometimes take a dive
Way down into the valley below.
And as I climb up that same road
I now have walked many times before,
I hear the ones who laugh at me say,
At last his faith will shine no more.

But when the praises grow louder still
They are upset and full of surprise,
And they are then ever so puzzled
As one thing they do not realize
Is that I am at the place and time
Where You indeed want me to be,
Because You have a future for me
Right next to You in eternity.

FORTY FIVE

You are never busy for me Lord
When I fall down on my knees in prayer,
And You never turn me back Oh Lord
When I come to You in my despair.
And sometimes when I cannot express
This anxious feeling I have inside,
I know I can put my trust in You
As my one and only faithful guide.

Then I open up my heart to You
And pour out all of my distress,
And offer You everything that I have
For wealth and power I do not possess.
Just a simple trust in Your promises
And the riches You have in store for me,
In heaven where my home is waiting
Where Your holy face will always be.

FORTY SIX

I was healed by Your afflictions
And no longer will I be condemned,
And not only You're my Saviour
But You also want to be my friend;
My comforter when times are tough;
My counsellor in times of need,
The provider of grace when I am weak,
Or should I fail in word or deed.

So why does my heart feel insecure
Against the problems of the day,
When I am in the grasp of Your hand
Each and every step of the way?
And I feel secure when I know
It is You who's holding my hand,
And then feel safer when I know
It's not the other way around.

FORTY SEVEN

You are the honour that I have left
In a world that's surely lost its way,
Where love and respect have both declined
And morals indeed have gone astray.
And people believe they can still find peace
While also mocking Your holy name,
And they pursue it in different ways
Perhaps in wealth or even fame.

But You alone are my perfect joy
The One who truly can fill my heart;
You provide me daily of Your peace
Of which the world was never a part.
For it's easy to know where to look
It's just a matter of priority,
To be truly humble and call on Your name
Would surely be the imperative key.

FORTY EIGHT

Take me into a deeper worship
To always be near Your holy place;
Let my prayers become like incense
As they ascend to Your holy face.
Grasp my hand don't ever let me go
So forever I am faithful to You,
Pour down of Your abundant grace
So that Your mercies are daily new.

Test my heart lest a flaw is found
In my dismal attempts to reflect Your grace,
Else take me, break me and make me new
That every blemish You would erase.
And when before You I shall stand
On that glorious judgment day,
My name is found in the Book of Life
And always beside You I will stay.

FORTY NINE

When I look back at my previous days
And throughout the journey of my life,
Through all the good times I was blessed with
And the sometimes endless days of strife.
I see Your hand in every corner
And every turn my life has taken,
Even when my sorrows were piercing,
Deluded to think I've been forsaken.

Though I never did much understand
The wisdom behind Your holy ways,
Why You consent for some to suffer
Even until the end of their days.
I know that I am never exempt
From the portion You have allotted for me,
Especially when my earnest desire
Was to be focused on eternity.

FIFTY

Had it not been for Your tender love
When You longed for me, to set me free,
And You came down from the heavens above
On the shameful cross to die for me.
Had it not been for Your healing grace
I would have been a stranger to You,
Would not have known Your forgiveness
And Your mercies that are daily new.

Had it not been for Your sacrifice
My future would've been dark and bleak,
Had it not been for Your guiding hand
And the times I waited to hear You speak.
Or the silent times You withheld Your word
So I could wait longer at Your door,
I would not have known You as a friend
Who will lift me up for evermore.

Had it not been for Your promises
That surround me every night and day,
And the peace that comes from deep within
Knowing that You will show me the way.
I would not have known You as a father
Who plans to lead me to success,
With a deeper knowledge of Your ways
And a future that You want to bless.

Part 2

THE JOURNEY

FIFTY ONE

I wonder what it is that You see
When Your testing eye is set on me,
How it is You look at me now
Compared to what You'd like me to be.
Do You see a fruit heavy with pride
Or someone eager to please Your heart?
Someone to prune all over again
Or from Your ways does not want to part?

What is it that You want from me Lord
And what results do You want to see?
Is my branch yielding adequate fruit
From the Holy Spirit that is in me?
Hear me Lord when I cry out to You
From the deepest corners of the night,
I ask You if there's a fault in me
Then let me be to Your own delight.

FIFTY TWO

When my own plans do not agree
With the plans You have set up for me;
When my efforts are all in vain
Like sailing against a stormy sea;
When all the windows are bolted shut
And it seems that there is no way out,
And the end result of my own ways
Refuses at last to come about.

With glee You watch from up above
Until I choose to release my hold,
Then gently You direct my way
That's when Your plans begin to unfold.
A road appears that I know I should take
And Your spirit in me assures my soul,
That now my journey can begin
And with You beside me, I'll never fall.

FIFTY THREE

When the road ahead appears to be
A hopeless task by any degree,
And over there, near the horizon
Where the path extends I cannot see.
A small step of faith is all I need
To start the journey I must make,
And discover just what lies inside
That road that I am destined to take.

The mountain that You asked me to climb
Gets bigger still with each passing day,
With every step it gets closer still
Now I'm afraid I have lost my way.
But You are beside me, Oh my Lord,
You are my strength and my guide,
The healer of my weak resolve
The shelter where I can always hide.

FIFTY FOUR

I see the cross, like a star it shines
Like a trusted beacon in the night;
Like a blazing sun in the dawn lit sky
With extended rays burning so bright.
And I wonder why that this would be
A cross that shines so plain and clear,
And it shines for none except for me
While I still don't have a sense of fear.

Is this a portent of things to come
Or a beacon that will guide my way?
I know I should not be asking this
Just keep on going from day to day.
And in time You will reveal Your plan
While I wait with patience at Your door,
Not knowing where that road may lead
Or what the future may have in store.

FIFTY FIVE

With a word You can make the mountains run
All hurdles to disappear from view,
Each day would be a chance for You
To show Your might in all that You do.
But how can I as a Christian grow
Should You thus decide to follow through
Where all would then be prepared for me
Without the need for heights to pursue?

The mountain there I now must climb
To see what is on the other side,
To see the riches You have in store
For those who dare to go outside,
And are not content to remain in place
And have chosen You as their trusted guide,
And rely on You when they follow the path
That leads away from the road that is wide.

FIFTY SIX

Oh Lord the path is getting steeper
And the skies have gone all dark and grey,
And the fog has now surrounded me
That I fear I might have lost my way.
But the cross is my beacon in the night
My guiding light in the bright of day,
My comforter in my time of need
My shelter from storms, come what may.

And even though the storms may come
To try and knock me from my path,
And shadows appear from the depth of night
Mocking me while they pour their wrath.
I am resolute, Oh my Lord,
For I am still focused on my goal,
To reach new heights in my walk with You
And in my quest to surrender my all.

FIFTY SEVEN

When the road ahead seems harsh and long
And I feel there is no end in sight,
And darkness has crept along the path
That barely now I can see the light.
And I feel empty and ever so weary
That I just want to abandon it all,
This is when I feel close to You
Especially when I can hear You call.

The cross is still there by my side
Shining its light so strong and clear,
Confirming to me the depth of Your love
Telling me that Your presence is near,
Encouraging me to be patient and strong
Guiding my path every step of the way,
That is when I resolve to go on
And keep my faith with every worn out day.

FIFTY EIGHT

My spirit cries out, come now my Lord
And take me to my heavenly place,
For there is nothing that can pick me up
Except the splendour of Your face.
When all around me is bleak and grey
And all I can do is sit and wait,
I sing Your praises in the night
And I wait in silence at Your gate.

For the path has become so rugged and steep
And there's an ill wind blowing strong,
And shadows unseen are knocking me down
Disturbing my pains all night long.
But I'm focused on that mountain top
Where many a saint have found their way,
Guided above by Your healing grace
And in Your rest they desire to stay.

FIFTY NINE

I look up to the skies and wonder why
You made me go on this quest at all,
That I am the one that You would ask
For total surrender when heeding Your call.
Now that I've been through testing times
Where often I would stumble and fall,
My enemies they are now rejoicing
And they talk of a god who looks too small.

But then You say, "My dearest son
I took you on purpose up that road,
Where no silver is found and surely no gold
Just a path that sometimes feels so cold.
But because I love you way too much
This is what I want you to know,
I could not let you stay where you are
And deny the chance for your faith to grow."

SIXTY

So what is it I am required to do
Before I can reach the Promised Land?
What are the steps that I need to take
Before I can see the works of Your hand?
Will You be my help when I am weak
Or when it's dark I cannot see,
Or pick me up when I am weary
Will Your grace be sufficient for me?

For the road is long and shadows abound
And I have nobody else but You,
The faith that I have in things unseen
Is simply enough to see me through.
And without this faith You cannot be pleased
That You may be my guiding light,
That shines on the path during the day
And brightens the darkness of the night.

SIXTY ONE

"I will always fix My eyes on you,"
Says the Lord of the stars in the skies,
"And My presence is there alongside of you,
This sometimes you don't realize.
My angels are there right by your side
Though your human eyes can't see,
And your progress up that mountain top
Is not up to you but to Me.

I will take you and lead you by the hand
Through dark and fearsome land,
And should you fall I'll be right there
So I may help you stand.
All you should do is keep on the move
With a firmness only you can find,
To keep your gaze on the mountain top
And never to look behind."

SIXTY TWO

Why does my heart feel heavy Oh Lord
When You are my strength and my guide,
Why is my resolve getting weaker still
When I have Your spirit inside?
Why am I then immersed in fear
When at present I should feel at ease,
Especially that I know You'll be here
When in prayer I fall on my knees?

For I am secure if I should fall
That You'll be here to lift me up,
And I truly know that should I thirst
You'll be here to fill my cup.
Is it because I fear the unknown
That sometimes I may trip and fall,
Or maybe through this faraway land
I have to take this trip at all?

SIXTY THREE

I wonder why it's dark all around
And light is lost without a trace,
When Your presence is here right by my side
And Your glory is shining in my face.
Why does my heart not feel at peace
When You are the Master of my soul,
And when I've learned how to let go
And how that I can surrender my all?

And then it hit me so loud and clear
And also without a shadow of doubt,
I figured out what I should do
And knew right out what it's all about.
For the light to shine on the path ahead
And brighten the corners of the way,
I need to reflect this light that comes
From the seat of Your throne without delay.

SIXTY FOUR

Teach me Lord how to be a mirror
To reflect Your light for all to see,
For all the creation of Your hands
Whether above or below the sea.
Let the likeness of Your glory shine
So all can see the spirit in me,
So that all can praise Your name
Now this to You is my earnest plea.

The light that shines will guide my path
And scare the nameless shadows away,
And then remove all traces of doubt
And turn my darkness into day.
Then all who don't receive Your light
For the lying one has blinded their eyes,
Can see the reflection of this light
And honour forever the Lord of the skies.

SIXTY FIVE

It's a wonder what this light can do
As it falls upon this desolate land,
It strikes with a sense of urgency
To light up the area on which I stand.
Now I clearly see the deep ravine
Just waiting to open beneath my feet,
Waiting so as to swallow me whole
Ending my walk in utter defeat.

But You are the God of the second chance
And You have a plan for my success,
You desire to give me a superior life
And the tools to deal with my distress.
And I thank You dearly for this truth
And the wisdom You give in times of need,
In order that You can show me the way
And help my journey to succeed.

SIXTY SIX

Lord bring me back to the point in time
When I lost the desire to reflect Your grace,
And lost my daily walks with You
And turned my back on Your holy place.
Was it a single enormous event
That shook my faith down to the ground,
Or I turned each day a little away
Then Your love was nowhere to be found?

Each day was darker than the day before
Just changing by a small degree,
And all of a sudden I was enchained
No longer the one who would be free.
Then You took me for a walk with You
So that my hope could be restored,
And You told me if I could persevere
I would finally receive my reward.

SIXTY SEVEN

Why do I feel so suddenly numb
That I wasted the best years of my life,
Instead of one in service to You
I chose this one that's full of strife?
You said to seek the kingdom of God
And all of this would be added to you,
Now I know how deep are these words
And just how much that they are true.

You told me, "I will compensate you
For the years that the locusts have eaten,
And I will heal and pick you up
If you're feeling downtrodden and beaten.
For all things are possible when you pray
With thanks for what you'll receive,
The answer will come in My own time
And this you'll need to believe."

SIXTY EIGHT

What else do You want to teach me Lord
While I'm in this walk with You?
For now I know all about the light
And what I need to renew.
With Your guiding hand I will carry this out
And endeavour to be a shining light,
A reflection of Your eternal grace
And Your beautiful face so loving and bright.

You said, " I Am, the light of the world
He who believes will not walk in darkness;
I am the One who conquered the world
And I plan to fully restore your gladness.
For I know the plans I have for you,
Plans not to harm but to prosper you;
To give you a hope and a future
And when you pray I will listen to you.

You will seek Me and you will find Me
When you seek Me with all of your heart,
And for now you're on your way
To a time when we are never apart.
I will give you wisdom along the way
As I take you up to higher ground,
I will guide you on the rightful path
And ensure that you are homeward bound."

SIXTY NINE

For a period of time I was lost in thought
Reflecting on what You have said,
And all the while my gaze was fixed
On that long and relentless road ahead.
Still on the horizon the mountain top loomed
Challenging those who dared to climb,
While mocking those who tried and failed
And were cast away from time to time.

But all of a sudden I was full of joy
When I knew that I had come this far,
And I knew that all I had to do
Was to keep pursuing that shining star.
With confidence now I truly can say
That everyone who have failed before,
Did not completely rely on You
And desired not to wait at Your door.

SEVENTY

And so it goes, there is always a time
For all events that we might face,
Events while some we can do without
Seem to naturally fall into place.
A time to love and a time to hate;
A time to laugh and a time to cry;
A time to mourn and a time to dance;
A time to be born and a time to die.

A time to build and a time to break;
A time to attain and a time to lose;
A time to be silent and not to speak;
A time to say whatever you choose;
A time to plant when the going gets tough,
And a time to sow in happier days;
A time to gather and one to discard,
Events that can happen in so many ways.

SEVENTY ONE

With a renewed zeal I continue the climb
Just so I can be closer still,
To my Lord and teacher on the way
While climbing yet upon that hill.
My inner strength is drawn from You
And the gentle words that You impart,
For You are the source of my content
And the One who can truly fill my heart.

And the light it shines much brighter still
Enough to elude the valley below,
Where the drop can be steep on jagged rocks
And some of the deepest rivers flow.
As I aim for the height where eagles fly
Where clouds are low upon the plains,
And above the clouds the sky is clear
And around the year it never rains.

SEVENTY TWO

While I am still under the clouds
The wind is fierce and the rain is strong,
From a distance I hear the menacing hounds
Emitting their howls all night long.
But You are my rock, Oh my Lord,
My shelter from the thundering skies,
From sudden turns along the way
From where the menacing shadows rise.

All of this is nothing compared
To the joy that waits on the mountain top,
And I must keep on moving still
For now is not the time to stop.
And I must now focus my gaze
On the blessings that are waiting for me,
When I'll receive my eternal rest
And I can claim in Your name the victory.

SEVENTY THREE

I cannot be focused on the road
When forces unseen are pulling me down,
Placing some hurdles along the path
Delaying me from receiving the crown.
And arrows of doubt are flying past
Aiming to plant a malevolent seed,
Though I did sustain a direct hit
My prayers were that they didn't succeed.

But I am for now a bundle of nerves
As I'm thinking now all hope is lost,
And I contemplate my retreat
And how I should minimize my cost.
And all of this would now become
Just a sweet and a blissful memory,
How I once tried to reach the top
And how I was close to eternity.

SEVENTY FOUR

It took the storm a very long time
To recede and disappear from view,
As I lay helpless on the ground
I had no plans as to what I should do.
And all of a sudden from nowhere came
A song I knew to my delight,
"Silent night… Silent night…,
All is calm… All is bright…."

From the direction where it came
I saw that the mountain seemed to glow,
There from the top a vision appeared
As if from two thousand years ago.
Angels were singing in the night
"To God in the highest, glory be,
And peace on earth, and goodwill to men,"
That was the message delivered to me.

SEVENTY FIVE

In the time I collected my strength
I was reflecting on the message sent,
The message for me was loud and clear
And I knew exactly what it meant,
God who's in the highest realm
Looked down upon our wretched state,
And put in effect His age old plan
Between Him and man He'd mediate.

And on that day a bridge was made
Between this earth and the heaven above,
And Jesus was born on Christmas day
An expression of the Father's love.
Now all that's required for me to do
Is to cross the bridge to reach the crest,
To reach the top there's no other way
This is the way that is surely the best.

Part 3

THE DISCOVERY

SEVENTY SIX

The moment that I enter the bridge
I feel as if I'm walking on air,
My feet are not even touching the ground
I look for the floor but it's not there.
I've become, it seems, a part of the bridge
Within its walls I'm free to run,
And I feel that I have just been born
As though my life has just begun.

I am immersed in a wonderful love
That a handful of words cannot portray,
This awesome thing I can't describe
There is nothing left for me to say.
A certainty that I'm homeward bound
Slowly starts to fill my soul,
The warmth of His awesome love
Fills my heart to make me whole.

SEVENTY SEVEN

I survey the walls along the bridge
They're full of words from ages past,
Some as said by the Lord Himself
Others as said by an ancient cast.
"For unto us a child is born
Unto us a son is given,"
This is what I found on the wall
This is what on the bridge was written.

And then I found even still more words
Written on some picture frames,
"Wonderful," "Counsellor," "Mighty God,"
Followed by some other names.
"Everlasting Father" next
And then there was "The Prince of Peace,"
The splendour was too much to bear
I had to fall down on my knees.

SEVENTY EIGHT

Christ the Lord, Glory of God,
Son of the Highest, Anointed One,
Word of God, Wisdom of God,
Him Who Sits on the Throne.
The First and the Last, Emmanuel,
God Almighty, Faithful and True,
Holy Spirit, A Child Born,
A Name Written that No Man Knew.

Many more names beyond compare
I saw inscribed along the walls,
And then I came inside a hall
Made up still of many more halls.
My eager heart was thumping fast
As I hurried inside without delay,
In amazement I saw along the wall
This truly splendid and fine display.

SEVENTY NINE

A majestic statue of a lion
Was the very first thing my eyes could see,
Since I was not expecting this
I wondered what this thing could be.
A statue so large it filled the room
It stood with authority in its place,
"King of Kings and Lord of Lords"
Were the words inscribed on its base.

The statue appeared to be so real
The King of Glory almost roared,
The King Eternal, The King Immortal,
The King who Comes in the Name of the Lord.
The King of Heaven, The King of Peace,
Blessed King of All the Earth,
A king He was while on the cross
And at the moment of His birth.

EIGHTY

In the second room I saw a calf,
An ox or a bull, it's all the same,
An animal designed for sacrifice
Whatever you want to call its name.
I marvelled at the paradox
The lion becomes the sacrifice,
On the cross to be slaughtered for me
Ready to die to pay the price.

The glorious Lion from the Tribe of Judah
Became the lamb and died alone,
The slaughtered lamb, The Lamb of God,
The Lamb in the middle of the throne.
The blameless and the holy One
By His grace He took the blame,
Then paid the wages of my sin
And gave His life on the cross of shame.

EIGHTY ONE

In the following room I saw a man
Holy and pure like no man can be,
Come to restore what man has lost
And in the process set us free.
For the Son of Man is come to seek
And also to save that which was lost,
The Last Adam, The Second Man,
Only as man He could pay the cost.

Seed of the Woman, Man of Sorrows,
Son of God, Son of Man,
He emptied Himself to be a man
Confined Himself like only He can.
Remained as God while on this earth
His glory now concealed from view,
And only then He could mediate,
Establish a peace, everlasting and true.

EIGHTY TWO

In the final room of this first hall
A majestic eagle was flying high,
He flew on top of everything else
So high that He could reach the sky.
King of Kings and Lord of Lords,
The Name Above Every Name,
The All and in All, Before All Things;
I Am That I Am, He would proclaim.

At the mention of His beautiful name
Then each and every knee shall bow,
Eternity past, eternity future
Time eternal, then and now.
Things in heaven, things on earth
Even all things under the earth,
Every tongue will then proclaim
His eternal dominion and His worth.

EIGHTY THREE

I entered into the second hall
And the words "I Am" were what I found,
And so I started to question myself
If I had missed what was profound.
And then the words they started to form
To finish the words displayed in part,
And they were written with neat succession
With only tiny breaks apart.

I Am the True Vine, I Am the Door,
I Am the Resurrection and the Life,
I Am the Light of the World,
The Way, the Truth, and the Life,
The Bread of Life, the Good Shepherd,
Each completed the words I saw,
Then it started from the beginning
And all I could do was watch in awe.

EIGHTY FOUR

The Hall of Faith was next in line
The faces were all of a long past time,
From Abel to Samuel the list was long
All were shown when in their prime.
Their faces were young and full of joy
With them the Lord was very pleased,
They came to Him and trusted Him
With faith they heard and they believed.

And without this faith it can never be
Possible to ever please the Lord,
For only with faith one can believe
That He exists and gives the reward.
To those who seek with all their heart
With faith have proof of things unseen,
For faith is the substance of things desired
At odds with what the past had been.

EIGHTY FIVE

Out of the corner of my eyes
I saw a section with my name,
Nothing there was shown inside
Some bookshelves in an empty frame.
My life has not been written yet
But still this part was kept for me,
Nothing was written about my past
Or what it was my identity.

The story is still not over yet
But still I could earn a mention here,
And to my surprise I also saw
Countless sections far and near.
All with names but vacant inside
Just waiting for the ending part,
A provision to choose if they are filled
Or suitably that they're torn apart.

EIGHTY SIX

In the following hall there stood a vine,
Pure and strong and reaching the sky,
And planted near the rivers of water
Where birds of the air can lodge or fly.
Just up from the roots were the words "I Am,"
"Abide in me, and I in you,"
The branches matured in all directions
That they obstructed the sky from view.

The righteous shall flourish as the branches
That grow so strong and they entwine,
But branches cannot bear fruit of themselves
Except that they abide in the vine.
And every branch that does bear fruit
Is purged that it may bring more fruit;
A branch that does not follow suit
Is cast to eternal disrepute.

EIGHTY SEVEN

It seemed that I have come to the end
Of this revealing and beautiful place,
And I was thinking how I would miss
Its splendid majesty and its grace;
The things I saw were nothing new
As all these facts were centuries old,
Except it was this time around
Unrivalled in the way it was told.

I turned to take a final glance
At the kingdom's secrets given to me,
But the scene had changed and now I could see
Images past from Calvary.
My Lord was dying on the cross
In agony there to set me free,
"Why have You forsaken me?"
I heard Him say this passionate plea.

EIGHTY EIGHT

I then observed the sins of the world
Being washed by the blood of the Lamb,
All of the sins, past and future
Placed on Him the great I Am.
And the image became so grotesque
That the Father had to turn His face,
The pain of the cross was then diminished
Compared to this that had taken place.

And then my Lord said, "It is finished,"
And then He bowed His head and died,
This wretched sight I could no longer stand
That I at once broke down and cried.
And when I later opened my eyes
I saw a figure of the risen Lord,
It only appeared for a little while
And then the image appeared no more.

EIGHTY NINE

With mixed emotions I turned around
And saw that there appeared a door,
I opened it wide with an eager heart
In a hurry to find out what's in store.
I saw the throne of the Lord up high
And a torrent of anguish filled my heart,
And this awareness came to me
I was undeserving of this sight.

And on the throne sat God Himself
The Father, the Son, and the Holy Ghost,
His throne was high and lifted up
And surrounded by an angelic host.
"Holy, Holy, Holy, Lord,
His glory fills the earth below,"
The smoke appeared as the angels bowed
This was truly a majestic show.

NINETY

The posts of the door moved at the voice
As the Lord of Hosts sent His command,
An angel then went down below
Carrying a live coal in his hand.
Headed towards a man below
Touched his lips and purged his sin,
His iniquity healed he praised the Lord
That now his ministry can begin.

And when the Lord said, "Whom shall I send?"
He stood up and said, " I am the one,"
The Lord said, " I have a mission for you
And this work shall indeed be done."
And so I said, "Send ME Lord,
I am the one whom you should send."
That was when I started to cry
For a time I thought would never end.

NINETY ONE

I found myself back on the hill
The moment that I opened my eyes,
Wondering if I was still alive
Or if I had truly met my demise.
I found myself in a different place
And the landscape I did not recognize,
And was this just a lucid dream
Or was it something otherwise.

And then I looked way down below
And found the spot where I had been,
Before I nearly gave up the fight
And thought that I could never win.
I looked up to the mountain top
It looked so close that I could see,
An outline of mysterious shapes
And the branches of a giant tree.

NINETY TWO

I heard the praises of the saints
Coming from the mountain peak,
And I heard a sweet rippling sound
Like water running in a creek.
Those flowing sounds from the top
Were just like music to my ear,
I understood the words they said
For they were all distinct and clear.

"Unto Him that sits on the throne
Blessing and honour, glory and power,
Unto the Lamb that was slain
Unto the Lamb for ever and ever.
For worthy is He God Almighty
Worthy is He the Lamb that was slain,
To receive the strength, wisdom and riches
Worthy is He again and again."

NINETY THREE

Suddenly as though a curtain had fallen
There was silence all over the land,
And I heard a shout, "How long before
Our blood You avenge with Your hand,
We who died for confessing our faith
As Your name we could not deny?"
Then silence came back and I heard a sigh
As though one was about to cry.

"I cry for the souls of those who are lost
For them I came down and died
To save them from a terrible fate
But then My name they had denied
And I cry for the things done in My name
In the present, future and past,
Those who are last shall be as first
And those who are first will be last."

NINETY FOUR

Jesus said,
"A greater love has no man than this
That a man lay down his life for his friends,
Though with a passion I hate sin
My love for sinners never ends.
I present to them the gift of grace
So they suffer not what they deserve,
But receive the riches that I give
The things that they do not deserve.

All has been completed and done
What's vital is they receive the gift
Of the cross and of eternal life,
Or else My punishment will be swift.
The time to open the seal is near
My anger will fall on those who stay,
As I take My own up to the clouds
When I come back on that glorious day."

NINETY FIVE

I heard the urgency of God's words,
Said with compassion for the lost,
A God that wants them to be saved
When He already had paid the cost.
Rejoicing not in the sinner's death
But that they turn from sin and live,
He has the means to give them life
And He has the power to forgive.

Now that I heard what the Lord has said
Where do I fit in His plan?
How can I serve my Lord and Master,
How can I do all I can
To spread His kingdom on this earth;
To bring the lost souls to His name,
So that He can heal the sick
And also take away their shame?

NINETY SIX

I clearly can see for miles and miles
As the dawn has now started to rise,
The fields that I see are ready for harvest
Bringing a teardrop to my eyes.
The fields are white for they are ripe
But I know the labourers are so few,
Those who'd bring the harvest in
With a heart that is devoted to You.

I fall down on my knees in grief
And to God above I say this prayer,
Make me a labourer for Your name
And touch the hearts of those who care.
To make disciples of all the people
Of all the nations of the earth;
To know You died on their behalf
And know how much the cross was worth.

NINETY SEVEN

"I'll never leave you nor forsake you,"
Said the voice from up above.
"I know exactly what you need
And I'll surround you with My love.
Seek first the kingdom of God
And all these things will be added to you,
For I am pleased to give you this
And the bread from heaven that is true.

I will restore the joy in your heart
For I have come to give you life,
That you may have it abundantly
And I will take away your strife.
I am the God of the second chance
I'll give you hope where hope is gone;
I'll give you strength when you are weak
And give you the will to carry on."

NINETY EIGHT

I look back and see what You have done
To take my faith to higher ground,
And all the things You let me know
And all about You that I found.
I thought my faith could withstand a storm
But this I need to recognize,
I used to hear from others about You
But now I've seen You with my eyes.

Now that I know You in this special way
I want to grow old by Your side,
To walk with You the rest of my days,
Your love to be my faithful guide.
To place my problems at Your feet
And lay my troubles at Your door,
To read the letters of Your love
And treasure Your words for evermore.

NINETY NINE

I never thought it would come to this
In all my years of being true,
I remember it like it was yesterday
When I said, "I give my life to You."
I had read about You in the Book
Of all the miracles that You had done,
You gave me life where the spirit was dead
But still I was Your baby son.

I grew in the spirit and in the truth
Under the guidance of Your hand,
You stood by me when I was lost
You tried to make me understand.
And even when I lost my way
You gently tugged me back to the fold,
You asked that I should write it down
And for my story to be told.

ONE HUNDRED

Thank You for the sunny skies
Though all around is dull and grey;
Thank You for my strength in You
Although my world has gone astray;
Thank You for the riches You give
Though I live from day to day;
Thank You for the joy inside
When You banish all my troubles away.

Thank You for the wonderful warmth
Beneath the wings of Your love;
Thank You for the sun and the moon
And all of the shining stars above;
Thank You for the triumph in You
Regardless of the treasures I lost;
Thank You Lord for taking my place
So I wouldn't have to pay the cost.

BIBLIOGRAPHY

1) Blue Letter Bible
   http://www.blueletterbible.org

2) Bible Treasures
   http://theeternal.biz/JCattributes.htm

3) Eternal Word of God
   http://www.ewog.org/namesofjesus.html

ABOUT THE AUTHOR

Ned Jacob spent his early years in Lebanon and received his secondary education at the International College in Beirut. He obtained a degree in electrical engineering from the University of Leicester in England, then moved to Melbourne, Australia where he spent twelve years, working as a city engineer.

The author moved to Canada and has since worked in a wide range of professions, including computer programming, teaching, home inspection, home energy evaluation and residential insurance appraisal.

Ned Jacob has been a Christian for over twenty years and has played drums in church worship for many years on a regular basis. He presented several programs on Christian values at the Melbourne Gospel Radio while in Australia. He and his wife Reem and their children Natalie, Andrew and Jonathan reside in Toronto, Canada.

Printed in the United States
40404LVS00002B/7-234